TECTONIC *SYSTEMS*

&

CHESS *PIECES*

BY TIM WALLACE

AUGUST 11-OCTOBER 14, 2012

LIBRARY HOUSE GALLERY

Curated by William Shelley &
Ericka Fernández

This catalog accompanies the exhibition:

Tectonic Systems & Chess Pieces by
Timothy A. Wallace

Library House Gallery
24164 Front Street
Grand Rapids, Ohio 43522
August 11-October 14, 2012

ISBN: 978-1-300-03220-5

Design, Layout, and Production by

William L. Shelley and Ericka Fernández

www.libraryhousegallery.com

art@libraryhousegallery.com

419.830.3080

Library House Gallery is a contemporary art gallery located in historic downtown Grand Rapids, OH. Its mission is to provide a space for emerging and established artists to express freely their creative expression.

Tim grew up in mid coast Maine in the small lobstering village of Owls Head. The texture of the rocky coastline and rich 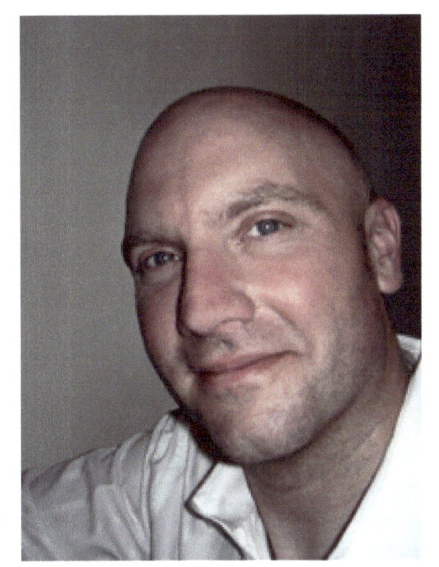 personalities of the hardworking community have continuously been strong influences on his work.

Tim attended the University of Maine where he studied Studio Arts with a minor in Education. During this time he worked for a local production potter, where his passion for wheel-throwing was indelibly sparked. Tim was enthralled by how a cylinder could grow and then expand outward into beautiful volumetric forms.

In 2000 Tim graduated from the University of Southern Maine, earning his Bachelor of Fine Arts Degree with a concentration in Ceramics. He then moved to Washington, D.C. to pursue a Master of Fine Arts Degree in Ceramics at The George Washington University (GWU), graduating with honors in 2003.

In 2001 Tim was awarded a graduate teaching assistantship, followed by becoming an adjunct professor at GWU from 2002 to 2004. During that time he also taught courses in ceramics and design at Northern Virginia Community College.

In 2004 Tim joined the faculty of the Ceramics Department at the Corcoran College of

Art and Design in Washington, D.C., where he is currently teaching.

Tim is "throwing" sculptural vessels on the wheel, to explore the volume, expansion, fluidity, and implied movement of the clay.

TECTONIC

SYSTEMS

The fragility of the ceramics medium can be seen as either an asset or a restriction. For Tim Wallace, this dichotomy is both. With Tectonic Systems Tim explores these dueling characteristics of clay and form, through a series of creation, deconstruction and finally reconstruction. Using these innate ceramic processes he has created a body of work that reflects the organic, aesthetic and historical nature of clay, form and earth.

The origins of clay as earth are explored through their relationship to shifting and transforming parts over a period of time. As clay ages segments of earth shift, reshape and settle. These natural phenomena reflect the human understandings of boundaries, faults, divides, movement and mapping. Tim explores these processes in order to better consider changes taking place when individual fragments begin functioning as a complete whole. He pushes this notion further by adding functionality to each form.

With this body of work Tim addresses the issues of control, or the perceived notion of control. Each form exists as a conquest of fear, reflecting certain liberation. They compel viewers to question ideas about change, adaptation, decision-making, responsibility, purpose, durability and death. Tim forces viewers to consider the things they deem precious, and ultimately question what they guard and cherish.

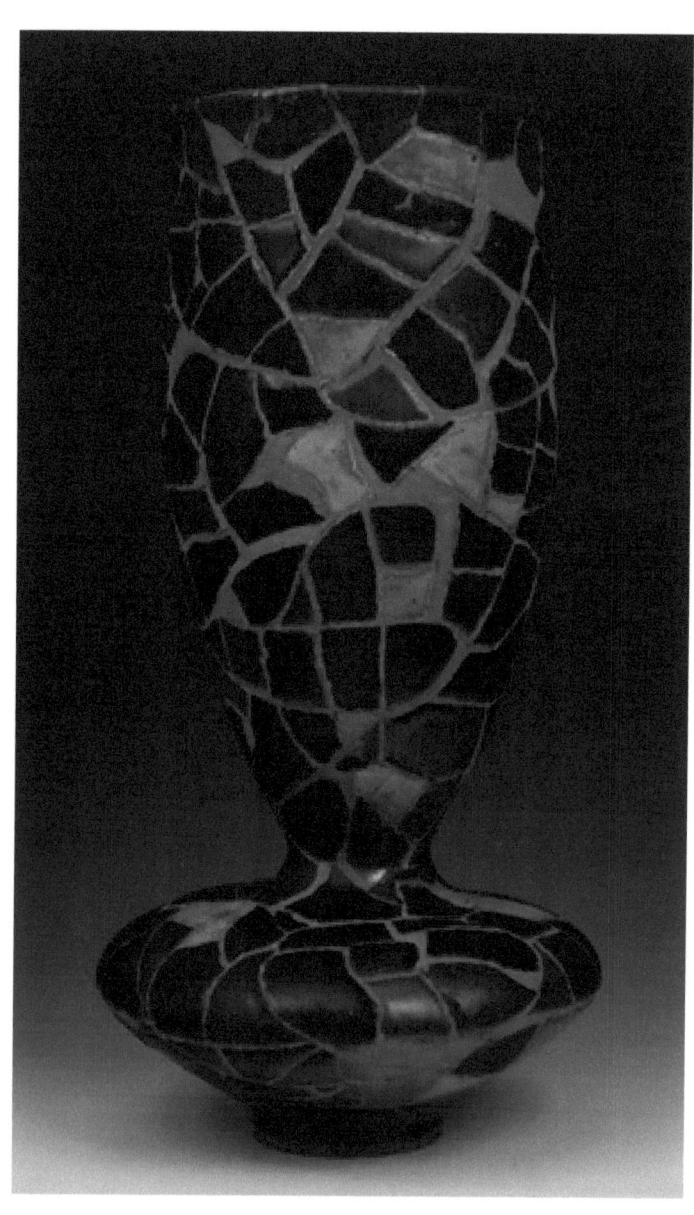

Black Terrane / 22.5" X 11"

Wheel Thrown
Stoneware
Reduction Fired Cone 10
Epoxies
Grout

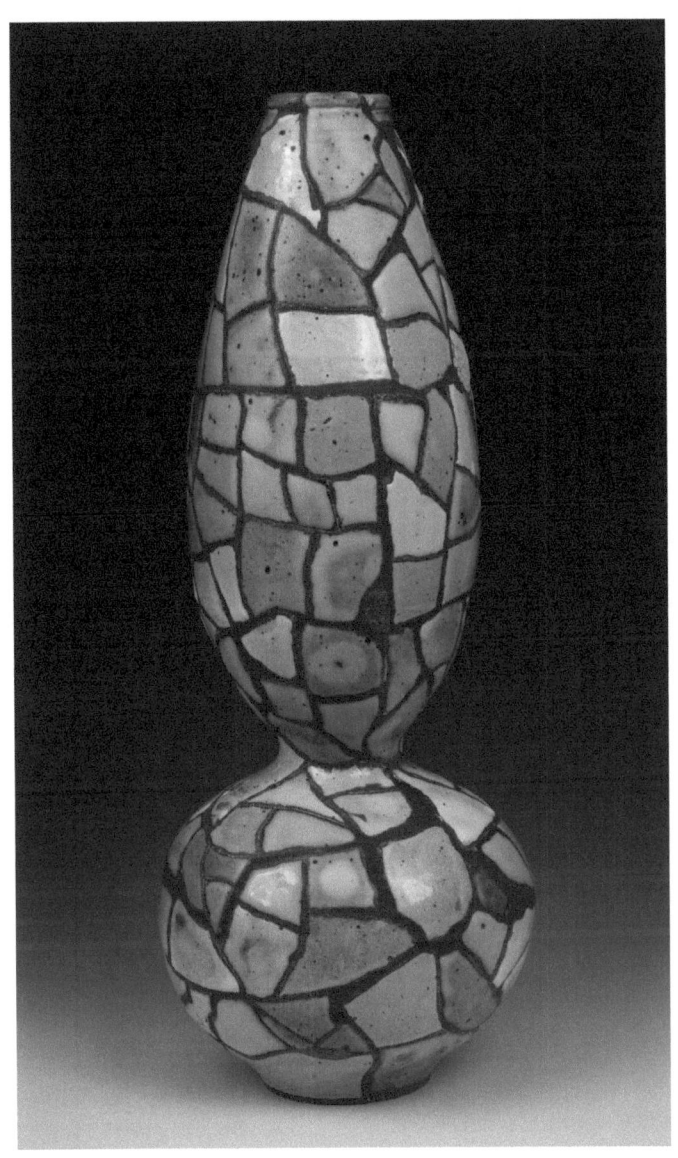

White Terrane / 22" X 8"

Wheel Thrown
Stoneware
Reduction Fired Cone 10
Epoxies
Grout

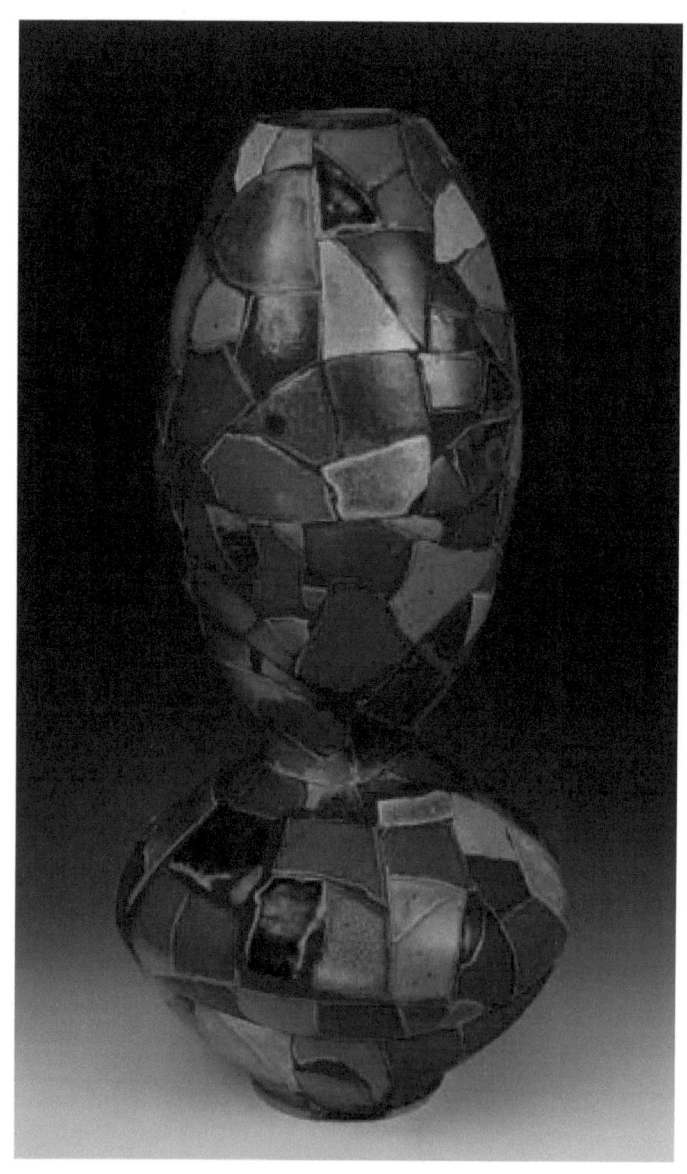

Blue Terrane / 24.5" X 10"

Wheel Thrown
Stoneware
Reduction Fired Cone 10
Epoxies
Grout

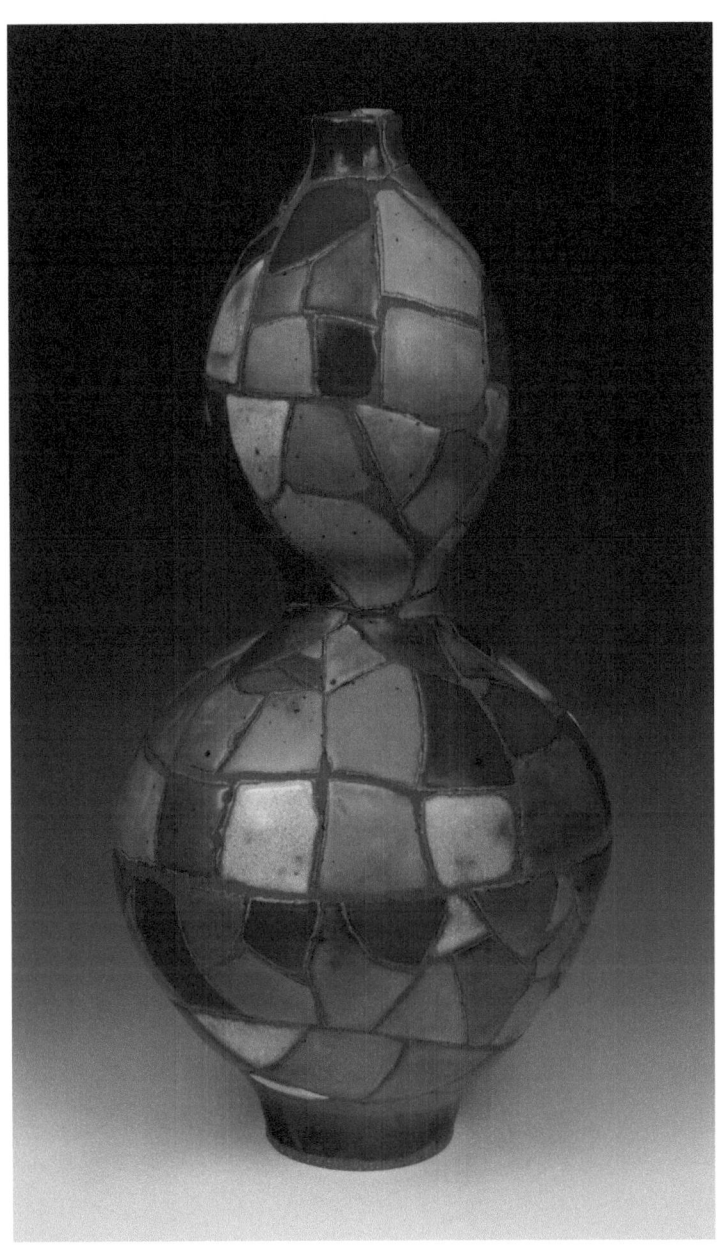

Purple Terrane / 21" X 11"

Wheel Thrown
Stoneware
Reduction Fired Cone 10
Epoxies
Grout

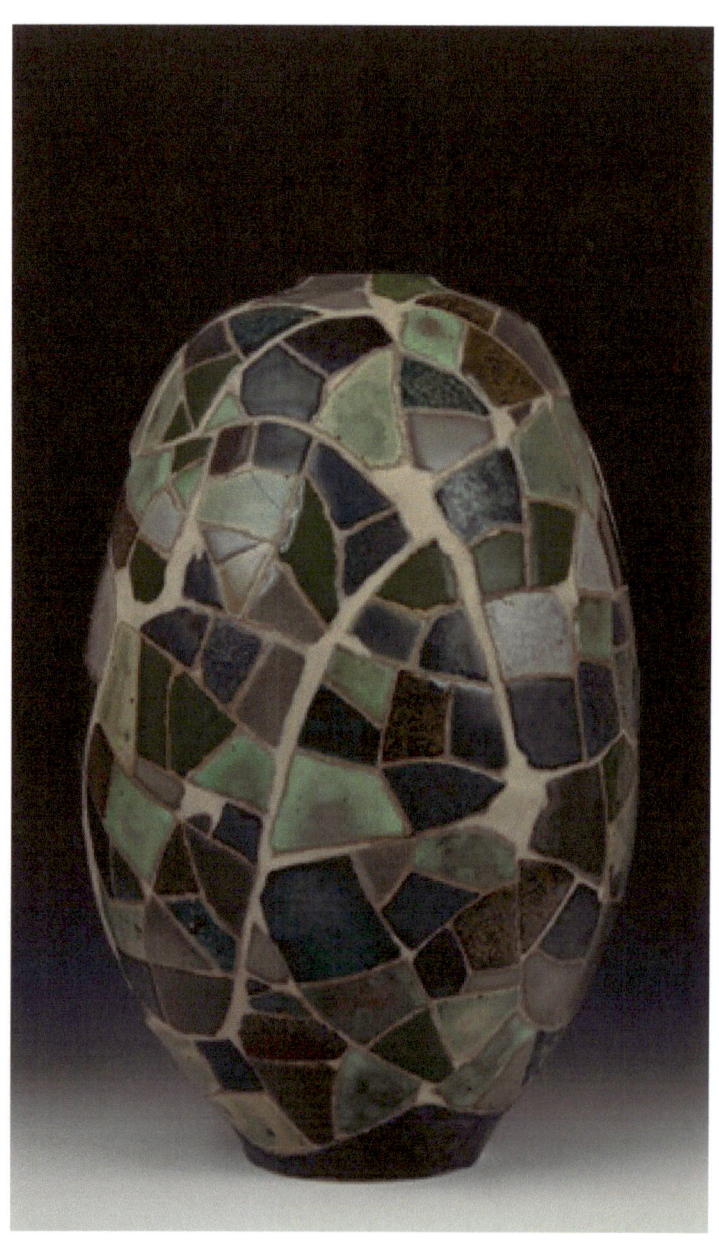

Green Terrane / 20" X 15"

Wheel Thrown
Stoneware
Reduction Fired Cone 10
Epoxies
Grout

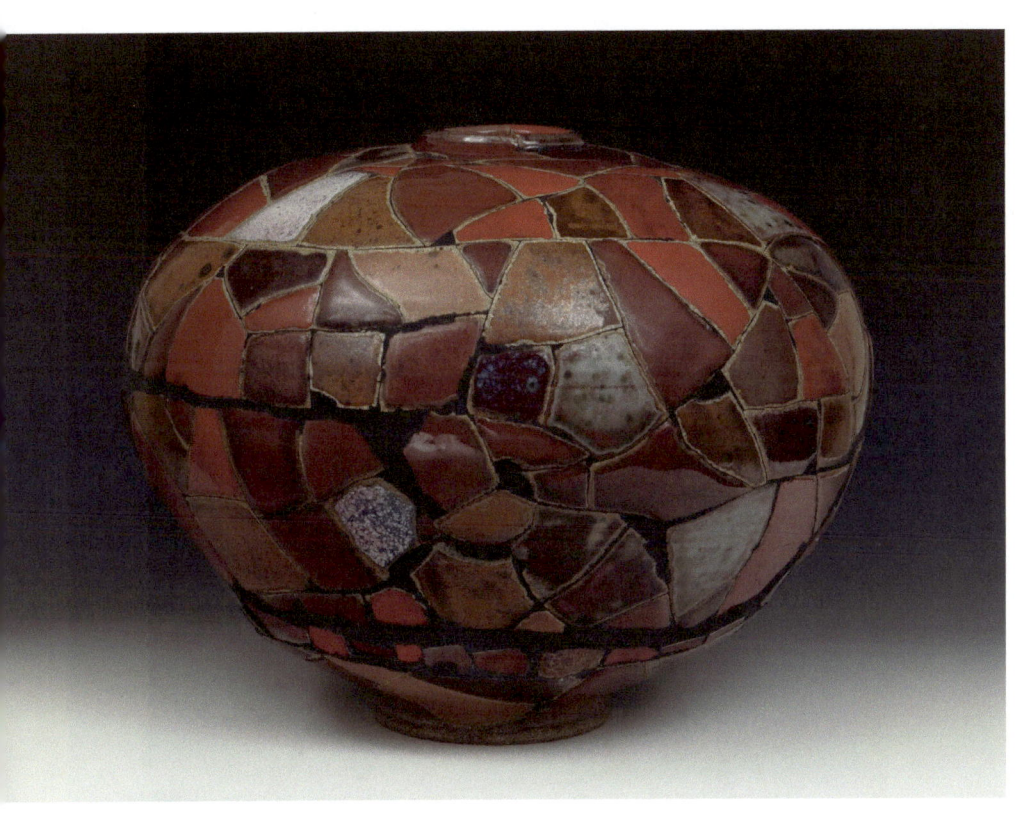

Red Terrane / 13" X 16.5"

Wheel Thrown
Stoneware
Reduction Fired Cone 10
Epoxies
Grout

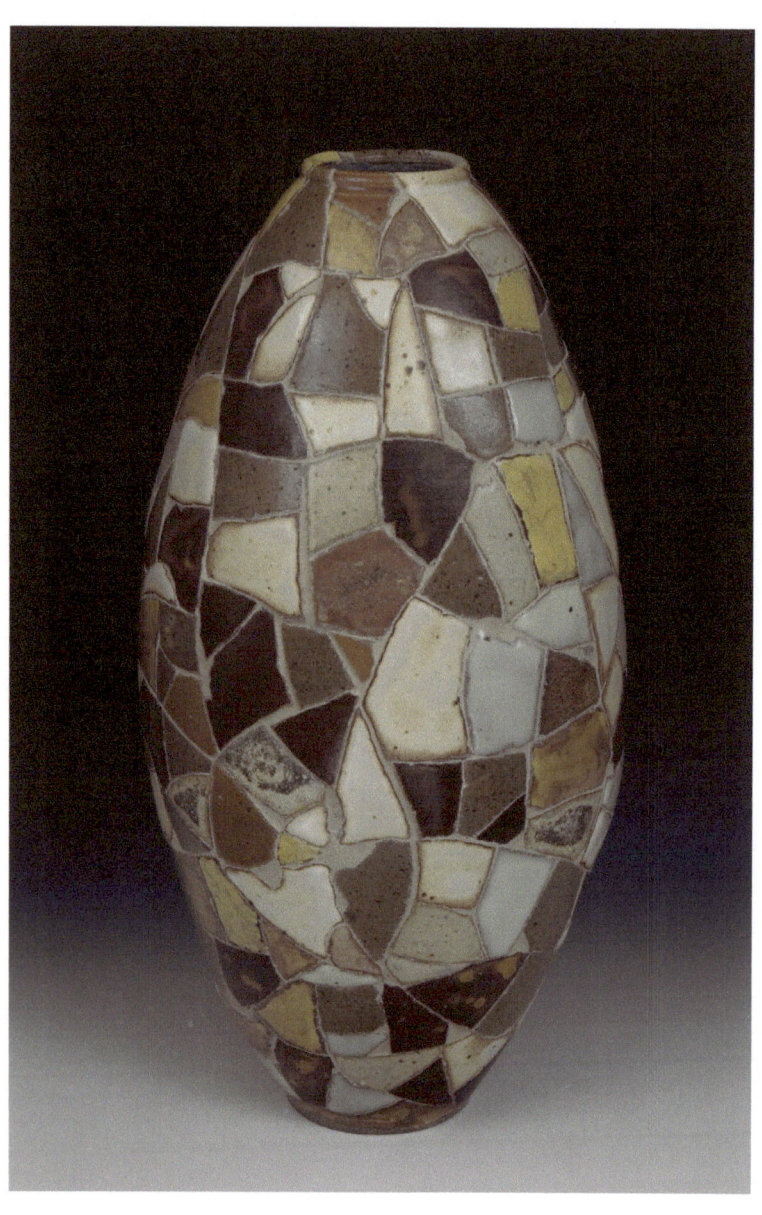

Yellow Terrane / 24.5" X 11"

Wheel Thrown
Stoneware
Reduction Fired Cone 10
Epoxies
Grout

14

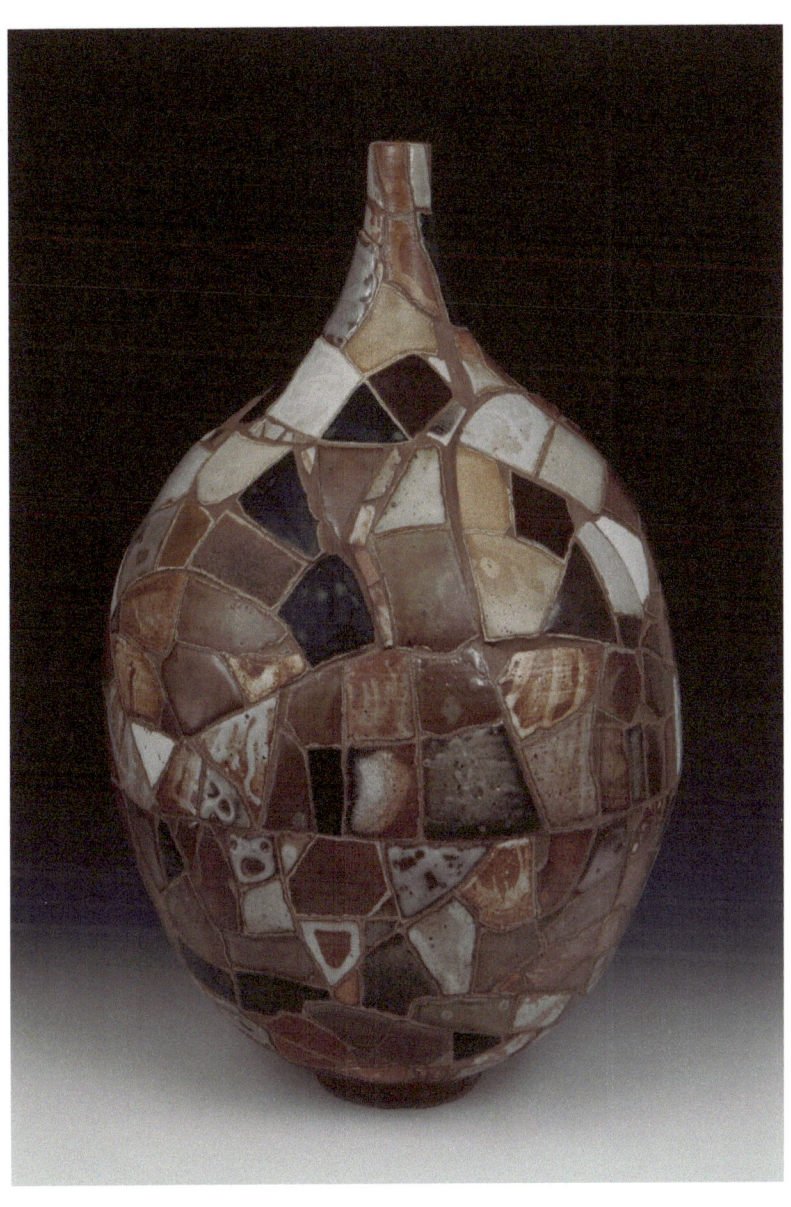

Orange Terrane / 24.5" X 14"

Wheel Thrown
Stoneware
Reduction Fired Cone 10
Epoxies
Grout

PROCESS

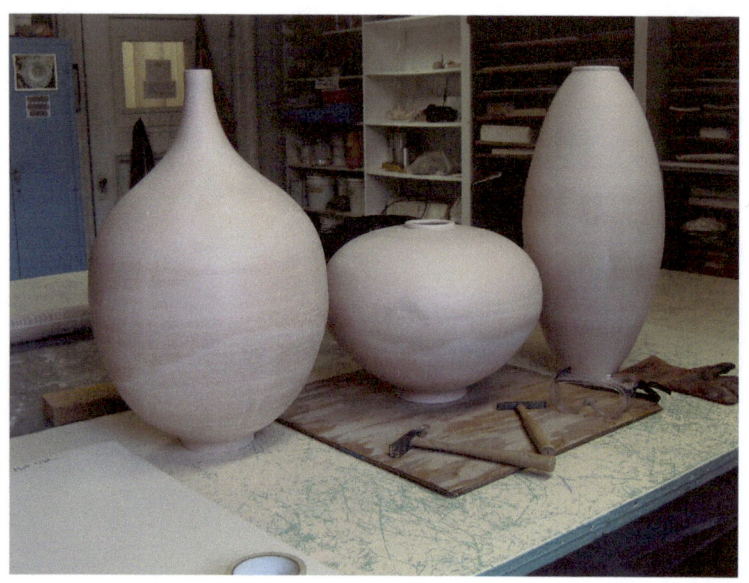

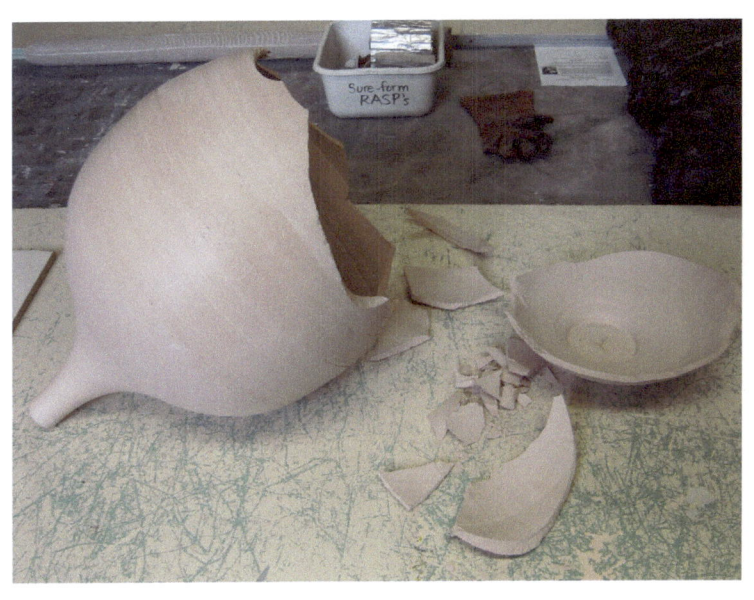

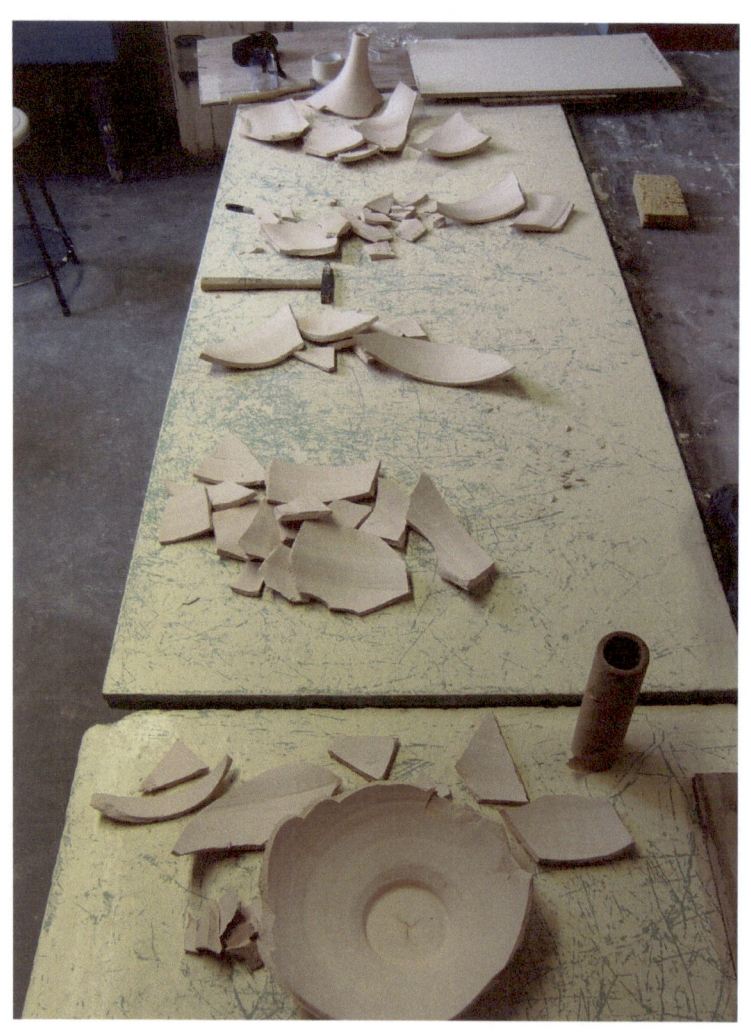

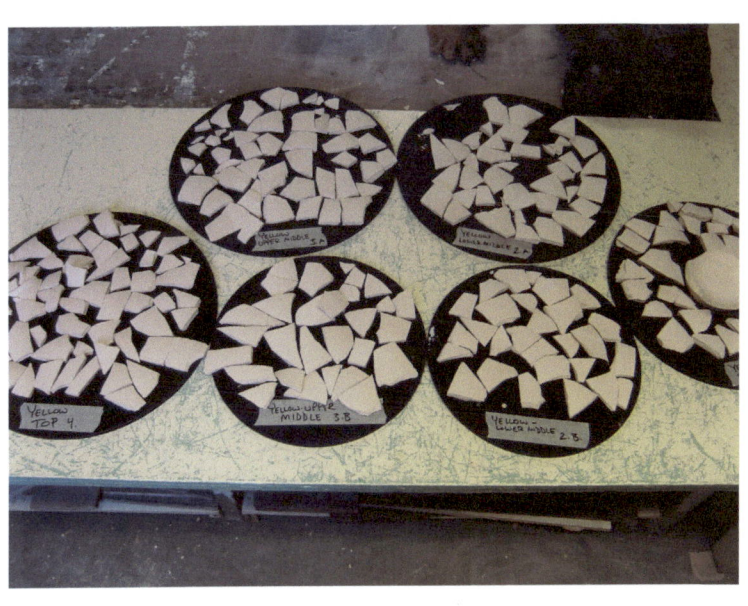

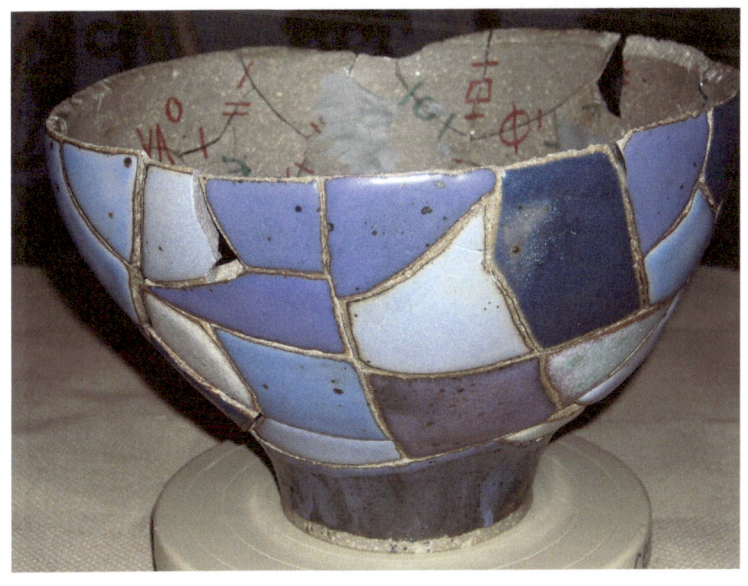

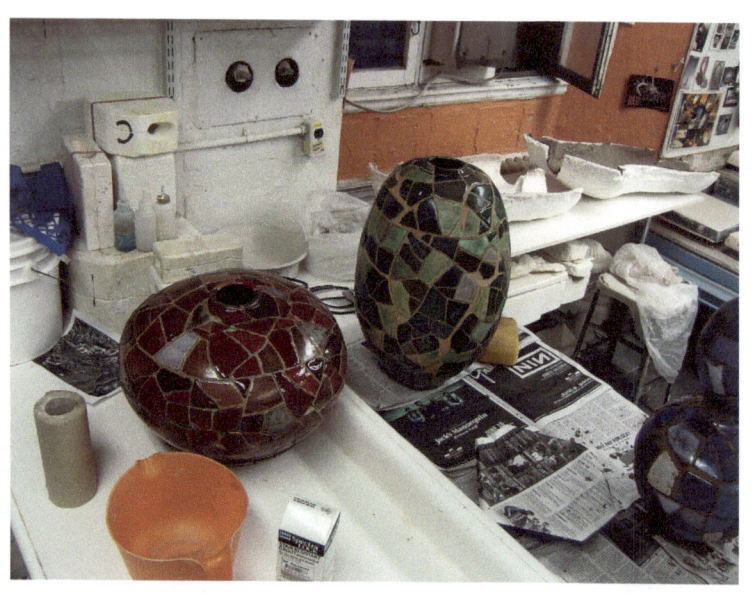

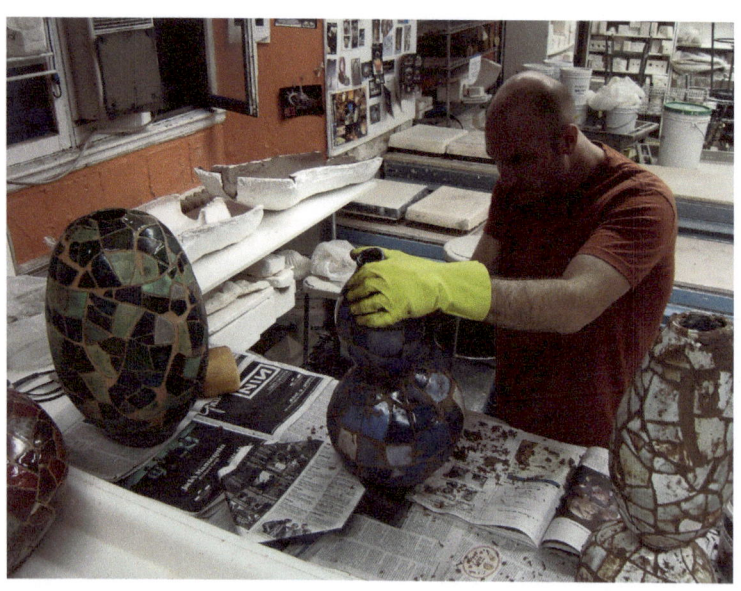

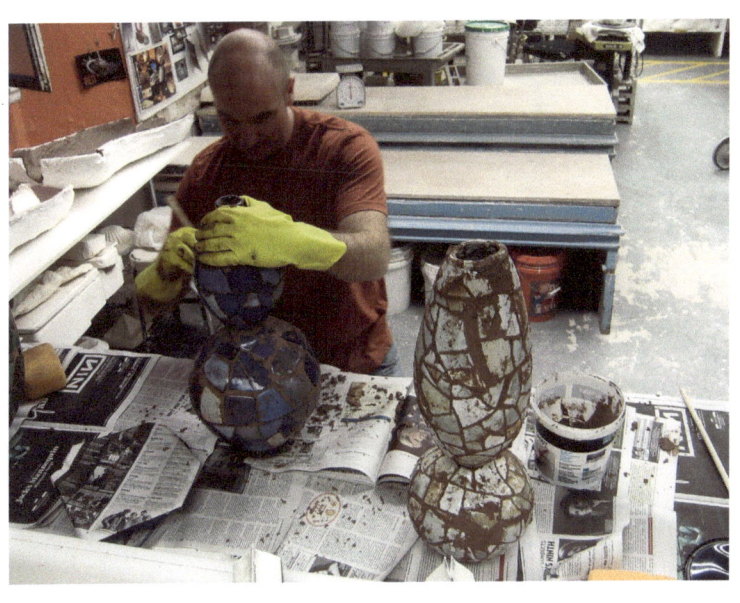

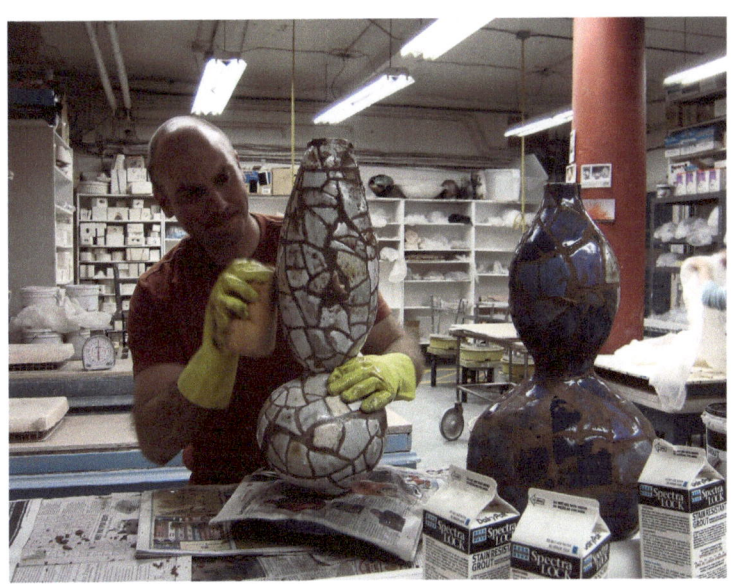

CHESS
PIECES

For Tim Wallace the symbolic nature of the traditional chess set has always been intriguing. However, the challenge of bringing something fresh to these forms could not be satisfied solely with the potter's wheel. As a result Tim has pushed the boundaries of these classical forms, as well as the limitations of inactivity and scale posed by singular wheel-thrown vessels. His romantic, highly-charged chess characters are somewhat abstract, but always suggestive and active.

Tim has injectd dynamism into the dormant chess forms, utilizing traditional wheel-thrown vessels. Their undulating throw-lines are adhered together to form limbs, and torsos, suggestive of human form. The scale of the forms underlines their presence and drama. Tim's Chess Pieces compel viewers to reconsider the game of chess and their own notions of heroism. This should include contemplating ideas of strategy, status, virility and vulnerability in a fresh and captivating way.

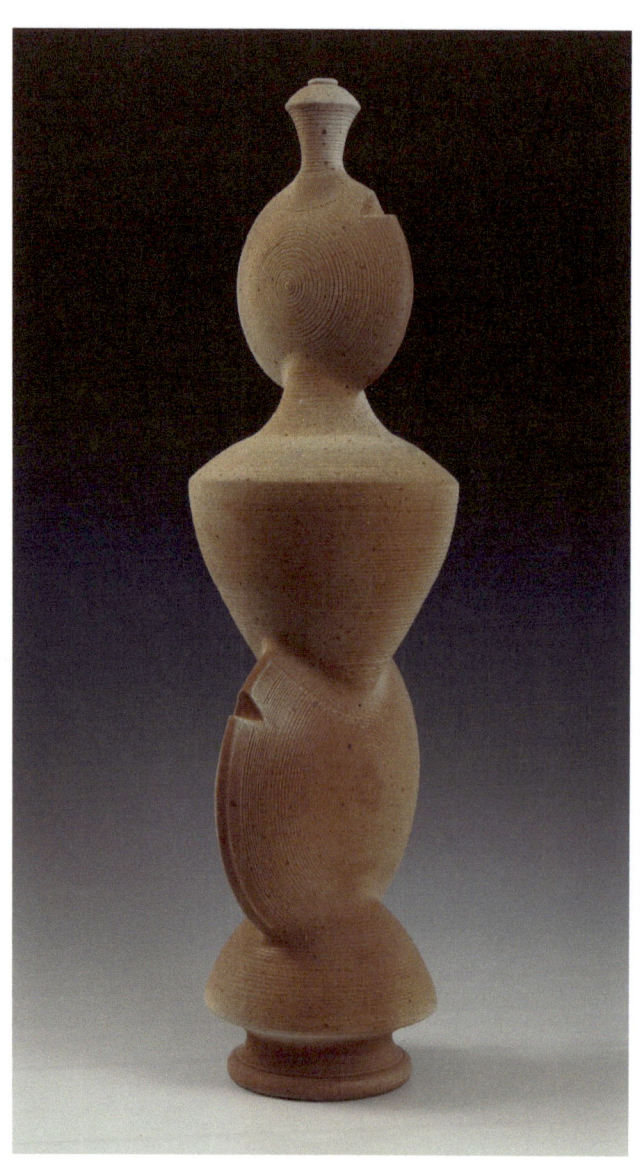

Bishop II / 32" X 11" X 10"

Wheel Thrown
Stoneware
Reduction Fired Cone 10
Shino Glazes

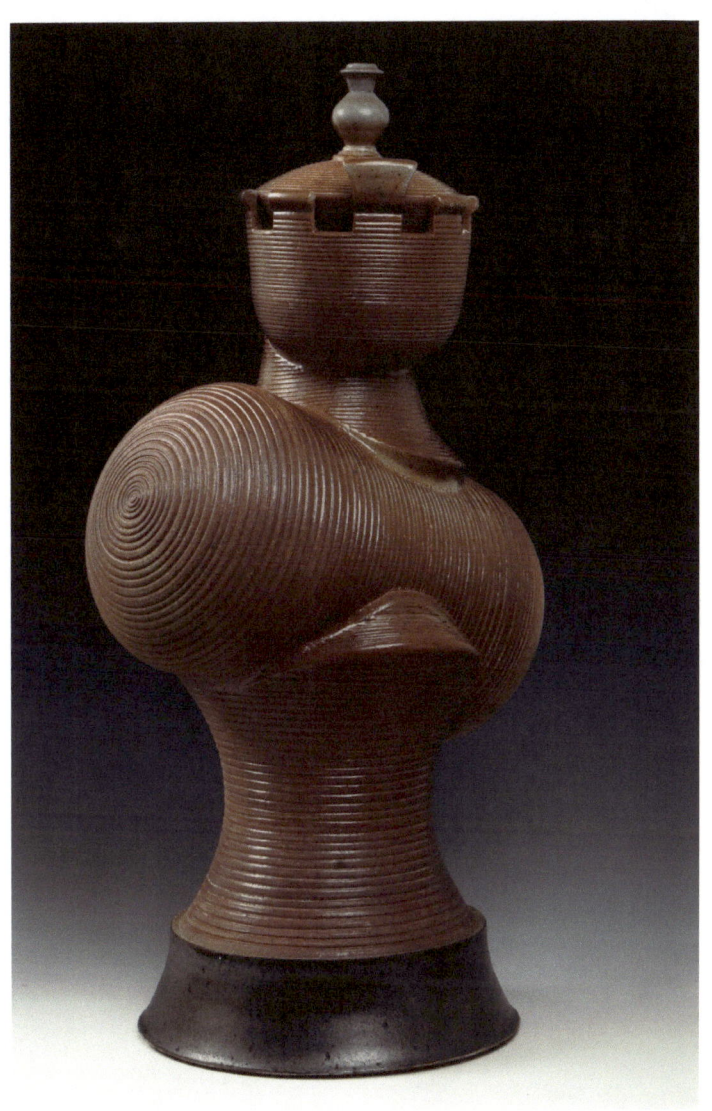

King / 33" X 16.5" X 13"

Wheel Thrown
Stoneware
Reduction Fired Cone 10
Shino Glazes

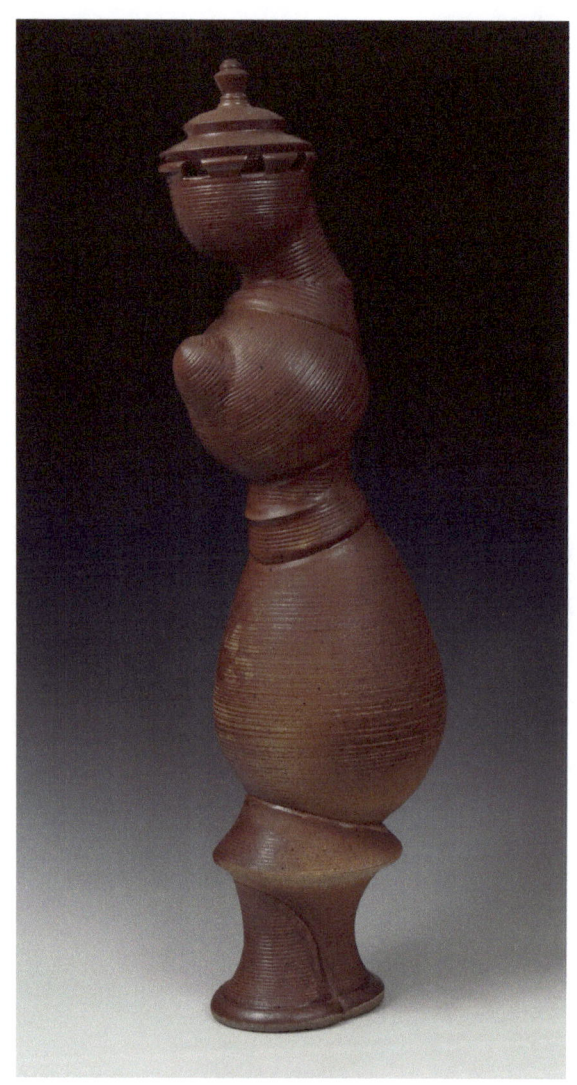

Queen / 37" X 10" X 13"

Wheel Thrown
Stoneware
Reduction Fired Cone 10
Shino Glazes

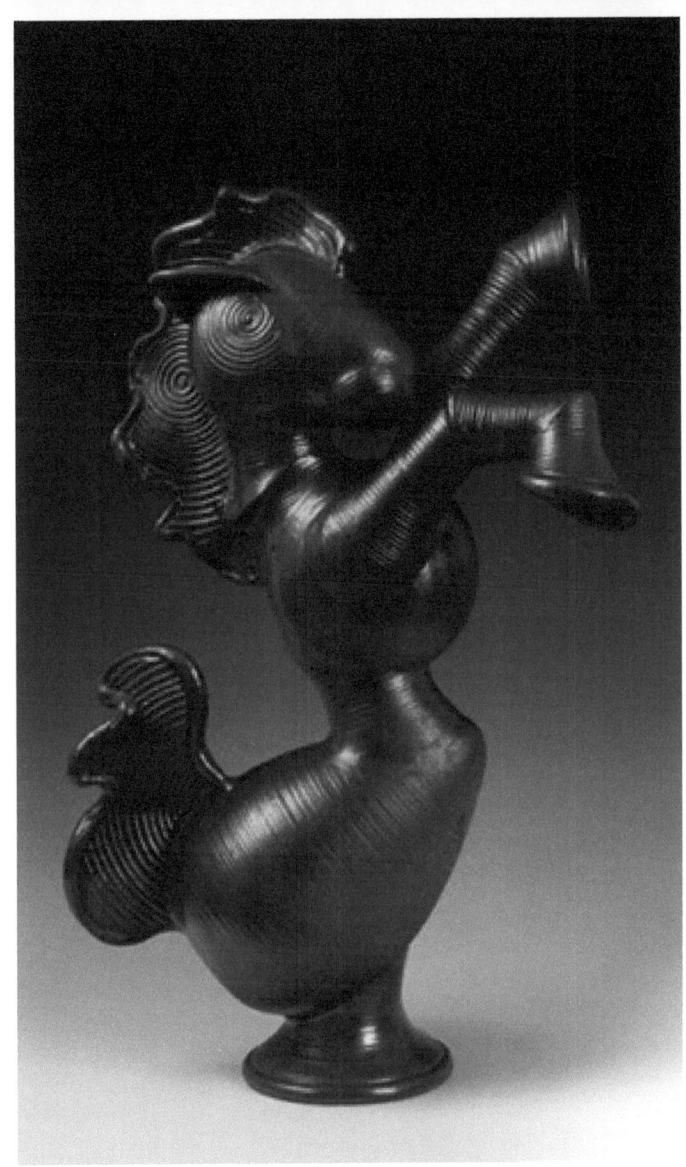

Knight / 23" X 10" X 16"

Wheel Thrown
Stoneware
Reduction Fired Cone 10
Shino Glazes

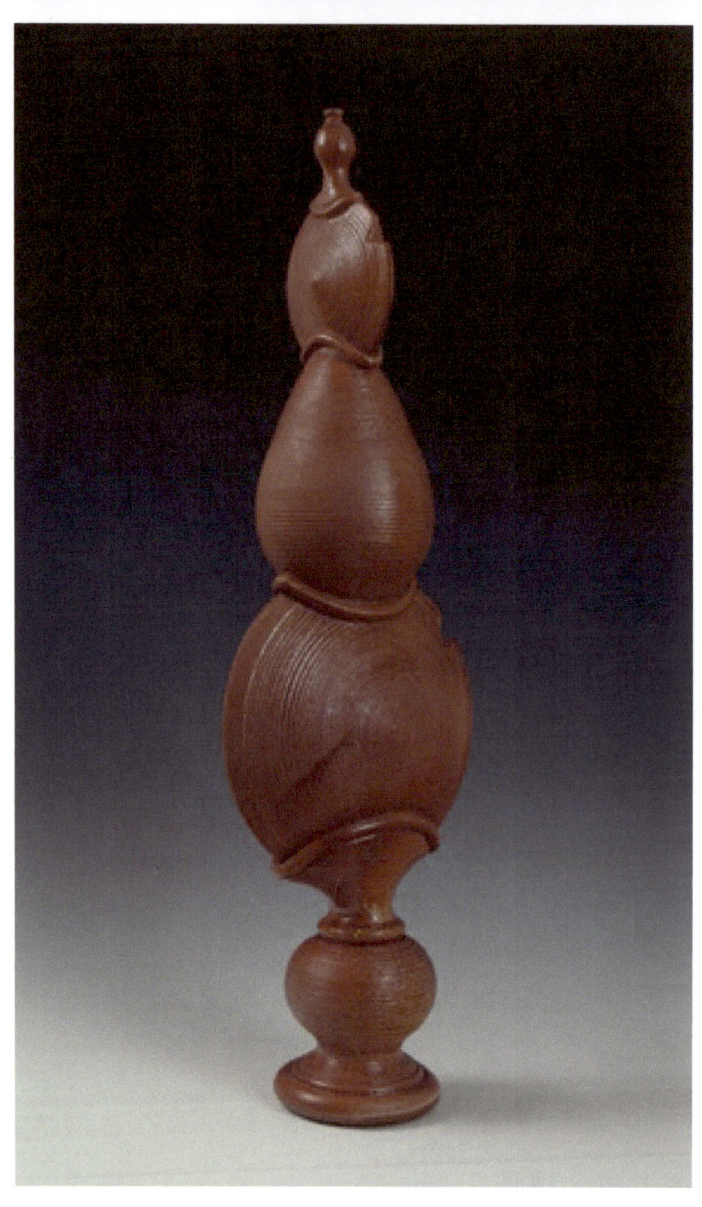

Bishop I / 30" X 10" X 7"

Wheel Thrown
Stoneware
Reduction Fired Cone 10
Shino Glazes

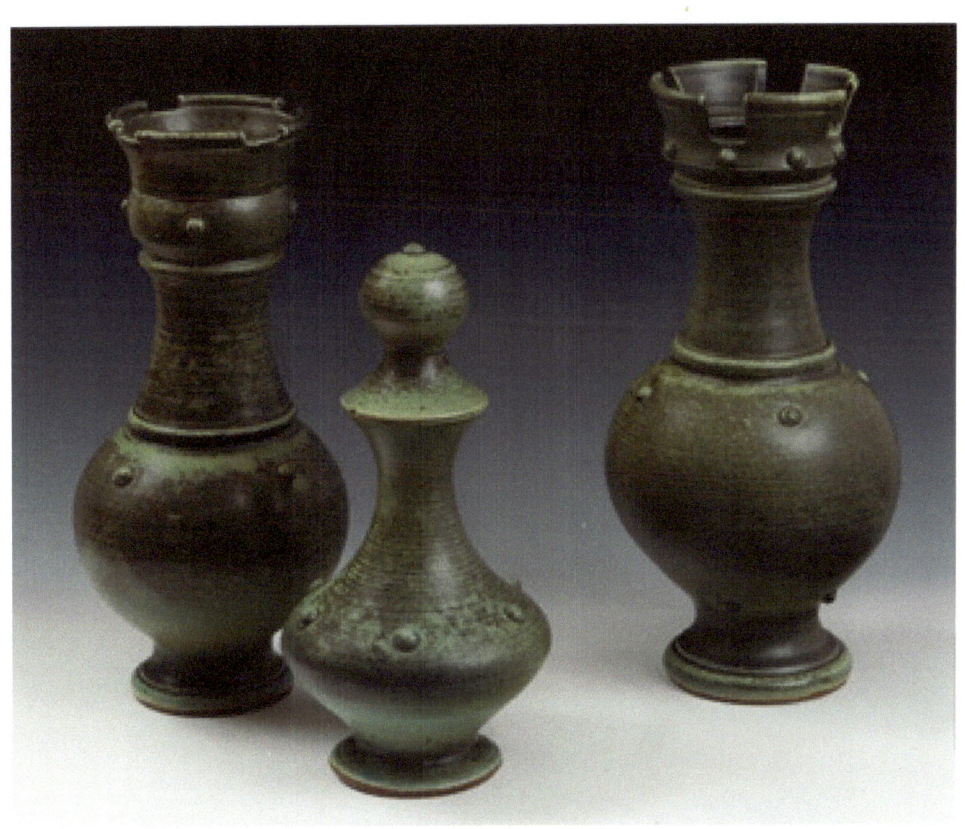

Rooks / 16.5" X 8"

Pawn / 13.5" X 7"

Wheel Thrown
Stoneware
Reduction Fired Cone 10
Patina Green Glaze

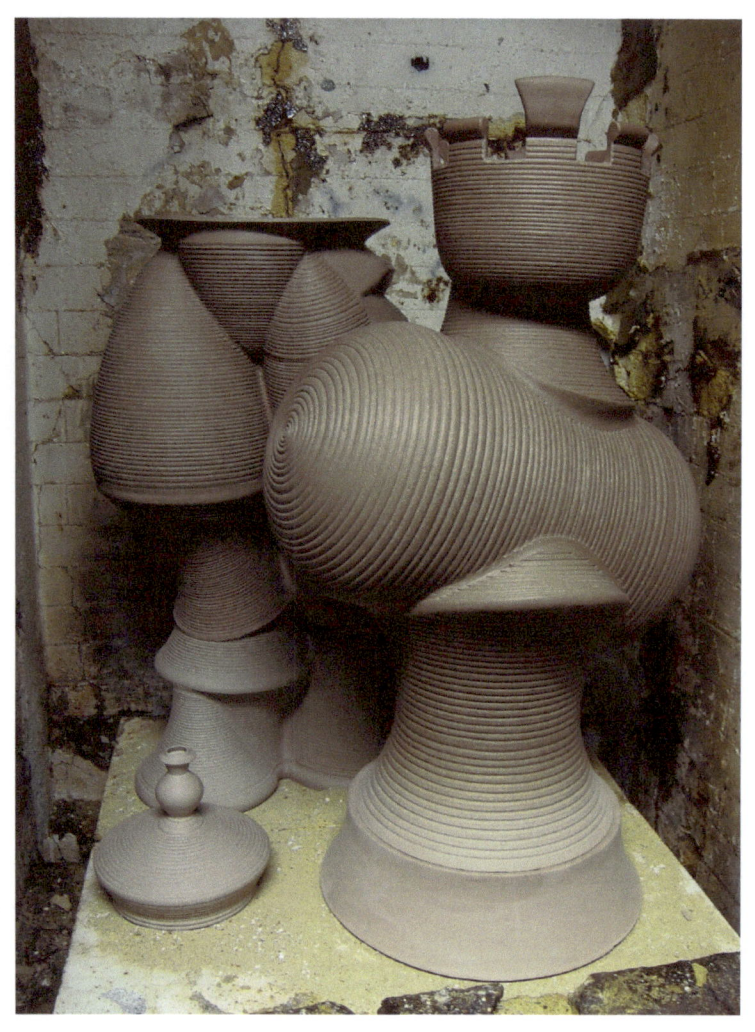

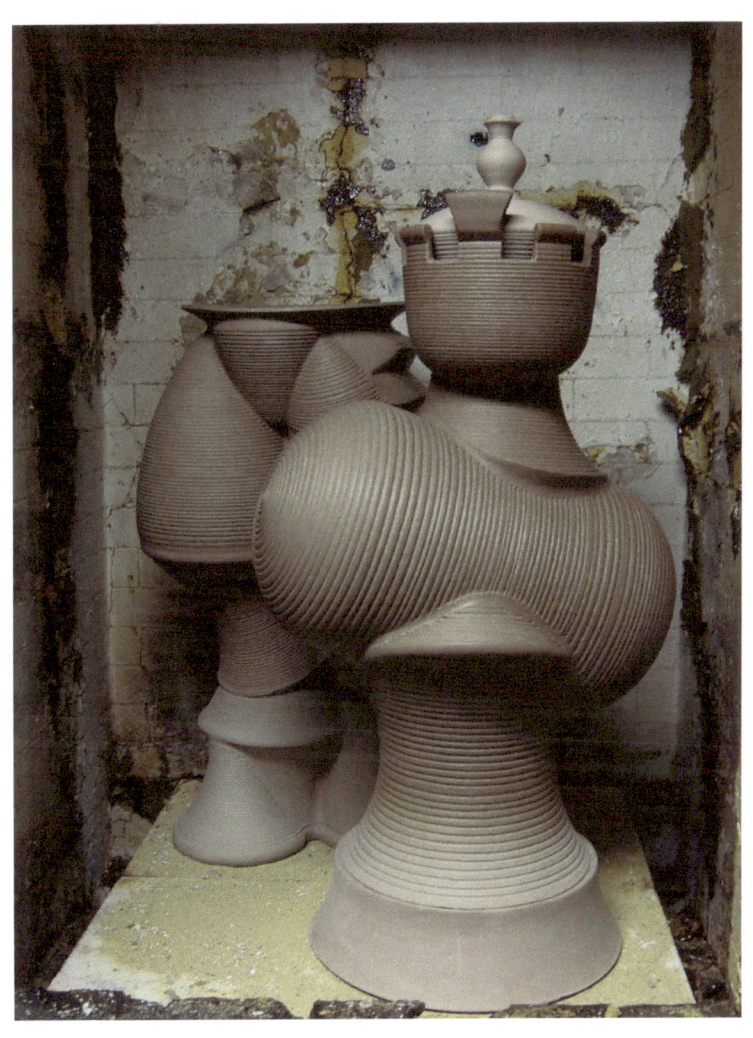

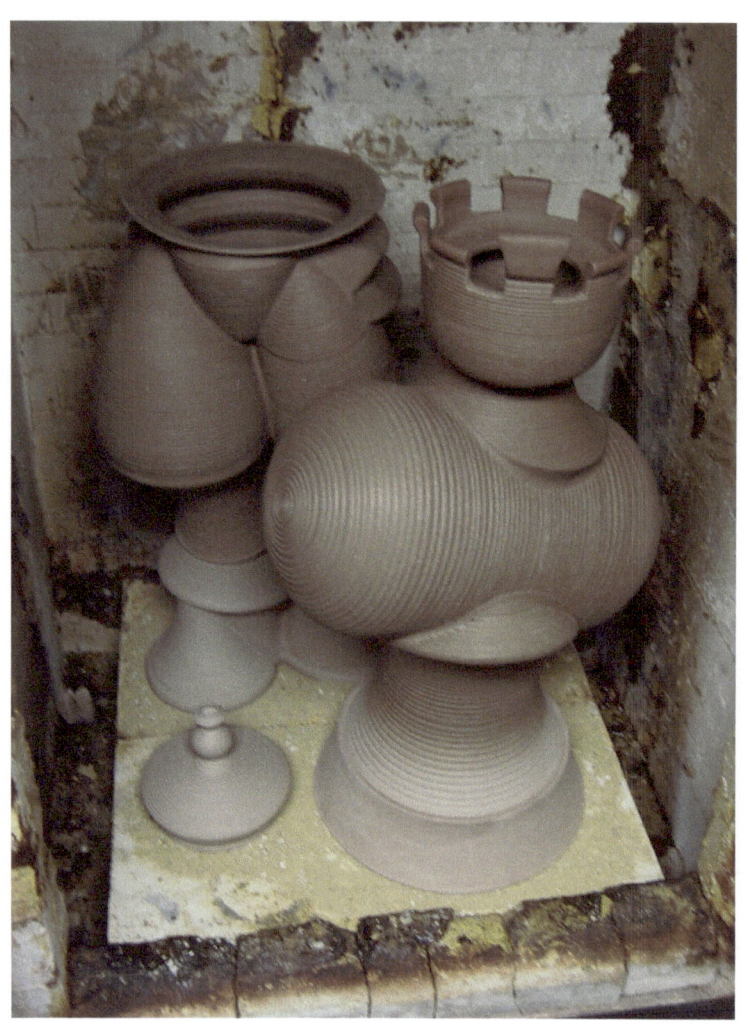

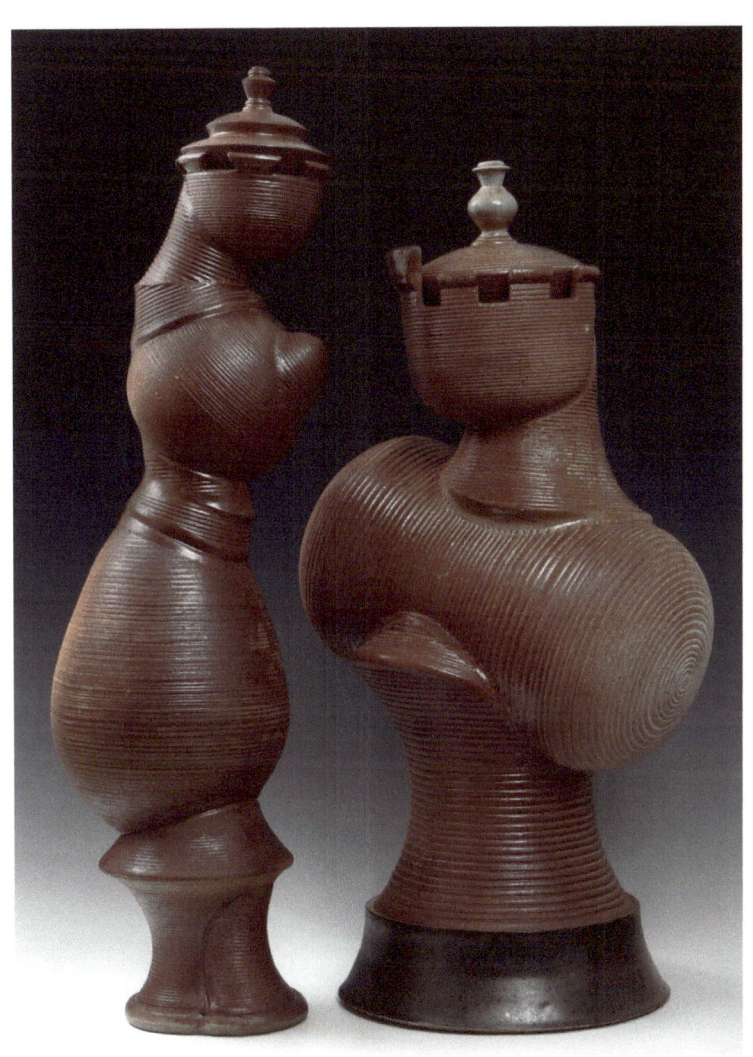

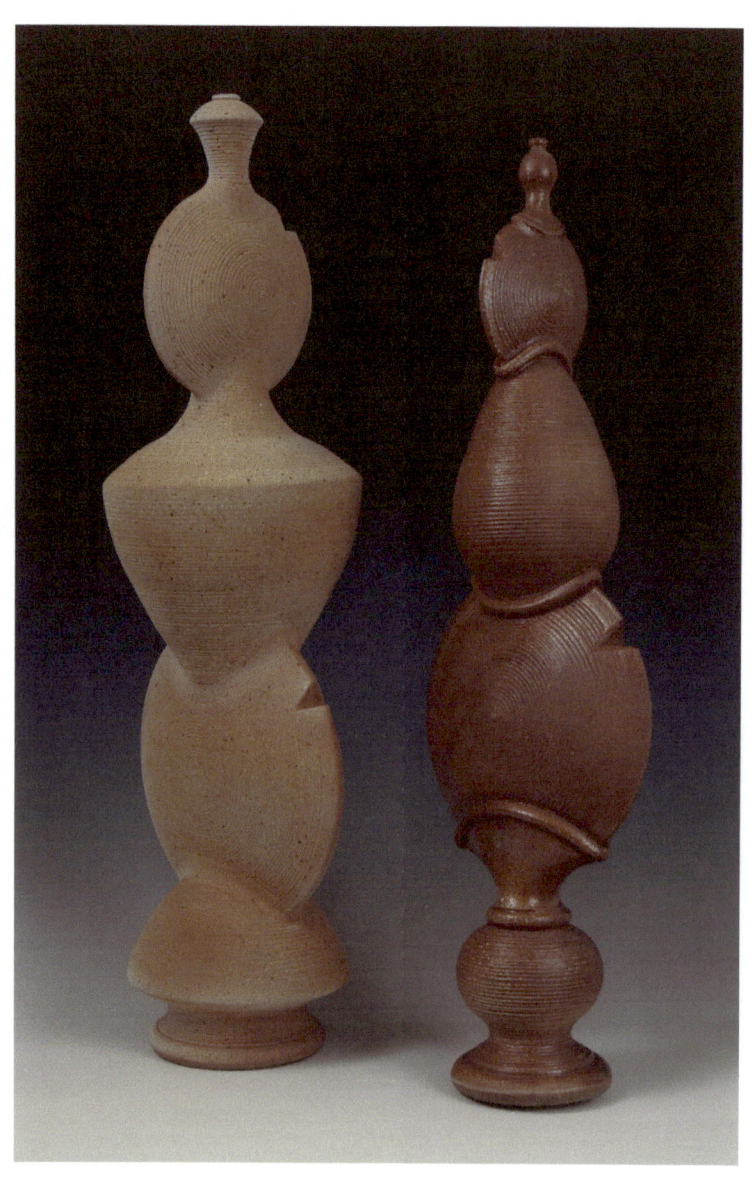

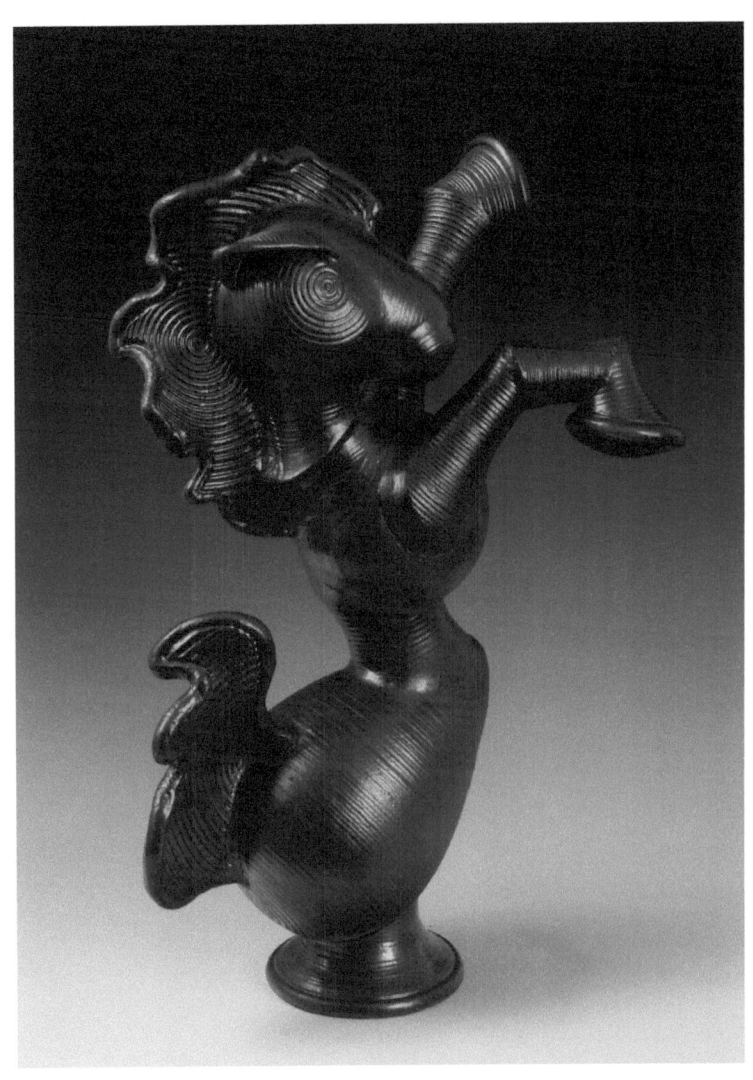

Education

The George Washington University Washington DC
MFA 2003 Honors GPA 4.0 | Ceramics

The University of Southern Maine Gorham, ME
BFA 2000 | Fine Art + Education

Employment

Corcoran College of Art + Design
Washington DC | 2004 - Present
> *Adjunct Professor* Introductory, Intermediate and
> Advanced Wheel Throwing, Introductory, Inter-
> mediate and Advanced Hand Building, Sculpture
> from the Wheel, Slip Casting, Mold and Model
> Making, Clay and Glazes, Pre-College Introductory
> Ceramics Workshops

The George Washington University
Washington DC | 2002 - 04, 2011 - Present
> *Adjunct Professor* Introductory Wheel Throwing,
> Independent Research, Graduate-Level Independent
> Research in Wheel Throwing

The Phillips Collection
Washington DC | Feb 2005 - Present
> *Security Operations Manager*
> *Lead Museum Supervisor* Sept 2004 - Jan 2005
> *Museum Assistant* Dec 2003 - Aug 2004

Northern Virginia Community College
Loudon VA | 2004
> *Adjunct Professor* Introductory and Intermediate
> Wheel Throwing, Introductory Hand Building,
> Ceramic Sculpture

Northern Virginia Community College

Alexandria VA | 2003

> *Adjunct Professor* Drawing I, Design II, Color
> Theory, 2- and 3-Dimensional Design

Landon School

(Independent Boys School K-12)

Bethesda MD | 2003 - 2004

> *Summer Art Instructor* Sculpture II, Ceramic
> Sculpture, Wheel Throwing

The George Washington University

Washington DC | 2001 - 2002

> *Graduate Teaching Assistant* (Turker Ozdogan)
> Intermediate and Advanced Wheel Throwing,
> Introductory Hand Building, Advanced Ceramic
> Sculpture

Group Exhibitions

S.O.M.E. So Others May Eat, (500 Bowls, Annual Charity Event)
Corcoran Gallery of Art, Washington, DC 2008-2011

Faculty Exhibition, Gallery 102, The George Washington
University, Washington, DC 2011

James McLaughlin Memorial Exhibition, The Phillips Collection
Museum, Washington, DC 2007-2011

Ceramics, Jewelry + Multimedia, Blue Fire Studios, Mount Rainer,
MD 2010

The Dimok Gallery, The George Washington University,
Washington, DC 2010

Hillyer Art Space, Washington, DC 2010

Smithsonian Craft Show, National Building Museum,
Washington, DC 2009

The Art of Tea, VisArts, Rockville, MD 2009

Chaos on F, Chaos on F Gallery, Washington, DC 2008

Collaborations, The Ninth Street Gallery, Washington, DC 2008

In Time, White Walls Gallery, Washington, DC 2007

Untitled, Anne C. Fisher Gallery, Washington, DC 2007

Sculpture Now! Washington Square, Washington, DC 2006

Summer Ceramics, Waddell Gallery, Loudoun VA 2006

In Flux, White Halls Gallery, Washington, DC 2006

Aromatic, Anne C. Fisher Gallery, Washington DC 2005

Admissions, Corcoran Gallery of Art, Washington, DC 2005

All Media Juried Show, Torpedo Factory, Alexandria, VA 2005

Faculty Exhibition, Corcoran Gallery of Art, Washington, DC 2004

Faculty Exhibition, The Dimock Gallery, Washington, DC 2004

Summer is Magic, Martin Luther King Memorial Library;
     Washington, DC 2003

Solo Exhibitions

Georgetown Courtyard, Washington, DC 2003

Visiting Artist/Demonstrations and Lectures

Gallaudet University, 2010

Northern Virginia Community College, 2009

National Student Portfolio Review, Pratt University, 2005-2007

Memberships

James Renwick Alliance (JRA) The Renwick Gallery of the
     Smithsonian Art Museum

National Council on Education for the Ceramic Arts (NCECA)

Washington Sculptors Group (WSG)

Society of American Mosaic Artists (SAMA)

Jurying

George Washington University Annual Student Show; Dimock
     Gallery, Washington, DC 2004

TIMOTHY A. WALLACE

510 21st St NW Apt 817

Washington DC 20006

twallace.ceramics@gmail.com

www.timwallace-ceramics.com

202.550.3825

Library House Gallery
24164 Front Street
Grand Rapids, OH 43522
419.830.3080
www.libraryhousegallery.com
art@libraryhousegallery.com

www.ingramcontent.com/pod-product-compliance
Lightning Source LLC
Chambersburg PA
CBHW041115180526
45172CB00001B/260